ARRIVE: A Reflection Jo

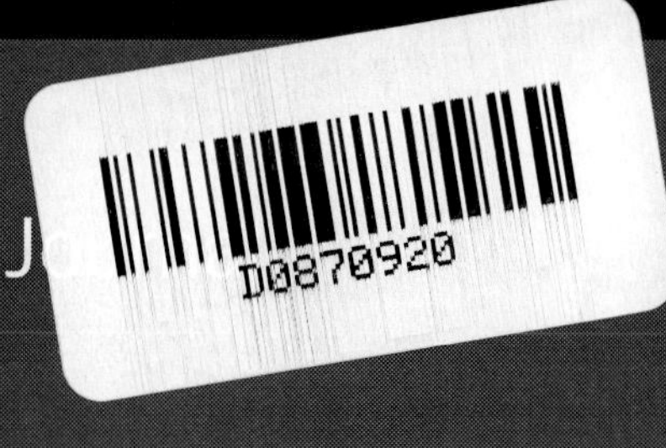

ARRIVE: A Reflection Journal

Amy M. Whited
and
Patricia A. Trujillo

Advanced Learning Press
317 Inverness Way South, Suite 150
Englewood, CO 80112
Phone (800) 844-6599 or (303) 504-9312 ▪ Fax (303) 504-9417
www.AdvancedLearningPress.com

Library of Congress Cataloging-in-Publication Data

Whited, Amy, 1965–
ARRIVE: assess, research, reflect, innovate, verify, evaluate : a reflection journal / Amy Whited and Pat Trujillo.
p. cm.
Includes bibliographical references.
ISBN 0-9747343-6-5 (pbk.)
1. Lesson planning. 2. Teaching—Aids and devices. I. Title: Assess, research, reflect, innovate, verify, evaluate. II. Trujillo, Pat, 1948– III. Title.
LB1027.4.W53 2005
371.3'028—dc22 2004062676

Printed in the United States of America

10 09 08 07 06 05 01 02 03 04 05 06 07 08 09

About the Authors

Amy M. Whited *has a broad spectrum of classroom experience. In her teaching career, she has worked with inner-city, at-risk elementary school students, as well as suburban/rural students. Her responsibilities as a classroom teacher involved developing and implementing curricula; creating a standards-based classroom; and collaborating with colleagues, parents, and administrators. Amy is an instructor with Metropolitan State College of Denver's Teacher in Residence Program. TiR is an innovative alternative licensure program that places teachers in high-need schools around the greater Denver metropolitan area. Amy also serves as an instructional coach.*

Amy Whited has a B.A. in Speech Communications from Auburn University. After spending three years substitute teaching, she returned to University of Denver, where she received her M.A. in Curriculum and Instruction.

Patricia A. Trujillo's *experiences within the educational community include working as a teacher, a staff developer, a principal, a supervisor, and an executive director of human resources. She is currently an instructor at Metropolitan State College of Denver. In each role, she always felt concern for the teachers who were new to a school. So many things happen concurrently at the beginning of the school year that those new to the building are frequently overwhelmed. Pat's hope is that this book will provide a structure for support, collegiality, and growth for new teachers and a blueprint for dialogue for mentors and administrators as they work with new teachers on their staffs.*

Pat Trujillo has a B.A. in Spanish with minors in Special Education and Psychology and an M.A. in Curriculum and Supervision. She has done postgraduate work with principal certification.

Contents

Preface

In our collective years, we have seen some remarkable teachers: on the cutting edge, creative, energetic, and continually searching for ways to have all students be successful. We have also seen our share of teachers who desperately needed to be doing something other than teaching. When we could, we counseled or weeded out some. Sometimes it was difficult; other times they knew that they needed to move on. Our goal was to provide students with teachers motivated to do their best: individuals who were reflective, willing to learn, and eager to grow.

This reflection journal is intended to make you introspective, to ask yourself the difficult questions, to seek out others who may be of assistance, and in some instances to see your world as others see it. It is our belief that the very teachers who use this book are the ones who seek and aspire to become better—and we congratulate you.

We want the world to know that many teachers are silent heroes. They are the providers of so much more than an education; they truly have their hearts, souls, and bodies on the line. In times that are demanding and require so much from each of us, we ask that you make the time to reflect on your successes and failures. We believe that through reflection comes growth.

We wish you well.

This book is written for every instructional leader. This preface outlines a few of the ways it can be used by:

- New teachers
- Veteran teachers
- Principals
- Department heads
- Team leaders
- Preservice teachers
- Student teachers

- Mentors
- College professors
- Specials or elective teachers

How to Use This Book if You Are a New Teacher

There are books that sit by a bedside and scream out to be touched and read. This book is designed to do just that. It is to be used to reflect on your teaching and as a journal to be read from time to time as your career continues. Reflection is a skill and a talent that is often overlooked. Yet, it can give us tremendous insight into why we stay the same; whether we are stagnating, treading water, or preserving a good status quo; and how we change.

Make some time each week to read and reflect on—in order—the variety of activities provided herein. Some are to be shared with colleagues; some are for self-reflection; others, such as Week 12, are focused on giving you a broader view of education.

How to Use This Book if You Are a Veteran Teacher

Week 31 begins with a quote from Ed Foreman: "If you always do what you've always done, you'll always get what you always got." This book will assist you with thinking about how you do things in the classroom and then perhaps how you could do them differently. Many of the prompts will assist you with thinking out of your comfort zone. Others will allow you to work with colleagues to whom you look up but with whom you have little opportunity to interact.

This is your journal. Select a week and continue with the process of growth and reflection. As you work yourself through the weeks, read back on the previous week and ask yourself if the reflections have provided you with cause to see yourself and your colleagues in a different light. Have you thought about introducing additional strategies? Going to a board of education meeting? Revisiting your lesson plans? Taking better care of yourself?

Appendix C contains a variety of tools that can be used not only in your own journaling, but also as a journaling lesson and tool for your students. As a result of your students' use of the tool, a discussion with your colleagues regarding the merits of journaling will be a opportunity for staff development.

How to Use This Book if You Are a Principal

This book has many applications for you as the instructional leader. For you and new teachers, each week can become a topic of discussion; this book and your journaling will serve as an ice-breaker between the two of you and provide insight and areas for growth. These are also terrific topics for your new teachers and their mentors. Each and every "Week" can be a topic for staff development and discussion.

This book can also be assigned, by you, to a mentor for a new teacher on staff. Indicators are that mentorships often fail because there are few guidelines for mentors. You may opt to select some or all Weeks as the mentor's responsibility and yet retain some as prompts for discussion between you and the new teacher(s) on staff.

Because most educators believe that reflection is an important component of self-evaluation, this book or a series of Weeks can be incorporated into the beginning-of-the-year goal-setting meeting between principal and teacher. The goal could be "self-evaluation" or "self-growth."

How to Use This Book if You Are a Department Head or Team Leader

Select the Week in advance, and have members of the department become familiar with its content before the department meeting. Then have a discussion: list strategies to explore for your specific content area, share rubrics, and don't forget "Week 20—Taking Care of Yourself." Self-reflection is a useful tool for evaluating your own success in your classroom.

How to Use This Book if You Are a Student Teacher or Preservice Teacher

Taking classes, seminars, and trying to feel your way into a new situation can be overwhelming. We often create a frenetic environment and do not allow ourselves to reflect. Take this time to journal your feelings, your successes, and things or areas that could have been done differently or better. At the end of the semester, take the time to look back on the growth you have experienced, the difference in your comfort level, and, most importantly, whether this is the profession that instills passion in your mind, heart, and soul.

How to Use This Book if You Are a Mentor

Mentorship programs often fail because we have not established specific guidelines and boundaries for mentor responsibilities. This book can very easily be used as a discussion point between you and your mentee. The book can be gone through systematically, Week by Week, or it can be used as specific events arise. It can also be used as the mentee identifies specific needs. We recommend that a specific day and time be set aside for mentor/mentee meetings.

How to Use This Book if You Are a College Professor

As you and your department members screen applications for student-teaching supervisors, you may find that the Weeks in this book are helpful in generating questions for the interview process. This book will also yield many discussion points if seminars are included in the student teacher experience.

Each Week can serve as an assignment. It is fascinating to observe how different settings stimulate a variety of results. The most useful purpose of an exercise of this type is to provide student teachers with exposure to a variety of scenarios, expanding their repertoire as they encounter similar situations.

How to Use This Book if You Are a Specials or Elective Teacher

With the exception of Weeks 22 and 24, all the Weeks in this book relate directly to specials or elective teachers. However, the situations are encountered routinely, so tweak a word or two and consider what you would do.

Standards in your content area specifically address the integration of content. Although in rare instances integrating some content may be a stretch, more often than not reinforcing the basics can and should be done frequently. Take a few minutes at the beginning of the year and develop a form that asks teachers in all grade levels, teams, or departments to provide you with a curriculum map for the year. Having the map will allow you to know what is occurring and plan lessons that complement student learning in other classrooms.

Rules, Routines, and Consequences

WEEK 1

The essence of knowledge is, having it, to apply it.

—Confucius

Action

Look at your school's discipline policy or handbook. Establish your own limits, taking the school's policy and procedures into consideration.

Reflection

- What did you do to introduce your rules, routines, and expectations?
- How did it go?
- What is your next step?
- How will you earn respect in your classroom?

Resources

Jones, F. (2000). *Tools for teaching.* Santa Cruz, CA: Fred Jones Publishers.

Wong, H. K., & Wong, R. T. (2005). *The first days of school.* Mountain View, CA: Harry K. Wong Publications.

District policy

School's discipline handbook or policy

Classroom Management I

WEEK

2

You don't do discipline with your mouth! If you did, nagging would have fixed every kid a million years ago!

—Fred Jones (2000)

An effective teacher is defined by Harry Wong as someone who has "positive expectations for student success, [is] an extremely good classroom manager and knows how to design lessons for student mastery" (Wong & Wong, 2005, p. 9). An effective teacher seems to do these things effortlessly, but in reality the class is very choreographed. You will need to go visit an effective teacher. Carefully examine the following elements and then reflect and respond.

Action

Be sure to take this assignment with you and write careful notes about the criteria listed here.

Classroom management

- Room arrangement
- Attention getters
- Expectations
- Procedures
- Routines
- Classroom rules
- General appearance
  —Is the room attractive, informative, and colorful?
  —Are there educational opportunities on the walls?
- Emergency procedures
  —Are they posted?
  —Are they easy to find?

Instructional strategies

- Are standards posted and/or observable?
- Is there evidence that the teacher is teaching toward a specific goal? If so, can you state what the learner will know and be able to do?
- Was there a warm-up? Did it serve as a launch for the day's activities?
- Did students make use of materials and resources?

Reflection

Reflect on the effective teacher's classroom using the preceding criteria. Comment on the teacher's classroom management. Try to use specific examples from the classroom. Comment on the teacher's instructional strategies, again using specific examples from the classroom. Finally, reflect on what you can implement in your own classroom based on the classroom you observed.

Resources

Cummings, C. (2000). *Winning strategies for classroom management.* Alexandria, VA: ASCD Publications.

Jones, F. (2000). *Tools for teaching.* Santa Cruz, CA: Fred Jones Publishers.

Marzano, R. (2003). *Classroom management that works.* Alexandria, VA: ASCD Publications.

Wong, H. K., & Wong, R. T. (2005). *The first days of school.* Mountain View, CA: Harry K. Wong Publications.

Classroom Management II

WEEK

3

> ***Calm is strength, upset is weakness. Or when in doubt, do nothing!***
>
> **—Fred Jones (2000)**

Action

Examine your classroom.

- Is your current method of discipline working for you?
- How do you react to good students who misbehave?
- How do you react to a student who continually misbehaves?

Reflection

Reflect upon how classroom discipline, rules, routines and procedures, *and* lesson planning fit together.

Resources

Jones, F. (2000). *Tools for teaching.* Santa Cruz, CA: Fred Jones Publishers.

Mendler, A., & Curwin, R. (1988). *Discipline with dignity.* Alexandria, VA: ASCD Publications.

Wong, H. K., & Wong, R. T. (2005). *The first days of school.* Mountain View, CA: Harry K. Wong Publications.

The Power of Body Language

WEEK 4

We need 4 hugs a day for survival.
We need 8 hugs a day for maintenance.
We need 12 hugs a day for growth.

—Virginia Satir (in Canfield & Hansen [1993])

Realize that body language is important. What you say when you speak is only one part of the message you are communicating.

How many times have you asked a student to do something when the child is sitting with his arms crossed in front of him? His voice may say yes, but his body language says "no way."

Action

Think about what messages you are giving your students with your body language.

- Do you use eye contact to communicate with students (*message:* I am really listening to you)?
- Do you walk around with your arms crossed in front of your body (*message:* I am not open to you or your ideas)?

Now, take a tally of your body language throughout the day.

- How many times do you use eye contact to communicate with students?
- How many times do you lean in to really listen to students?
- How many times do you stand with your hands on your hips?
- How many times does your face reflect your frustration?
- Does your body tense up when a student misbehaves?

Reflection

- What value do you give to the idea that body language is a powerful communication device?

Reflection *(continued)*

- Can you think of an instance when you felt like you were following the correct steps in carrying out a disciplinary action, only to have the student turn around and do "it" again?
- Now think about the body-language portion of that occurrence: what part of your body language do you think might have been giving a signal different from your words to that student?
- Other than the classroom, where might body language be important in terms of your professional career?

Resources

Canfield, J., & Hansen, M. (1993). *Chicken soup for the soul.* Deerfield Beach, FL: Health Communications.

Jones, F. (2000). *Tools for teaching.* Santa Cruz, CA: Fred Jones Publishers.

WEEKS

5 and 6

If you don't know where you are going, you can't get there.

—Jon Saphier and Robert Gower (1997)

Action

With a colleague, examine the state standards. Decide how you will organize the standards and benchmarks for the year. Over the next two weeks you are going to create a curriculum map.

- Do you agree that the essential elements of your subject area have been identified? Why or why not?
- If your district has a curriculum map in place, how do you ensure that you are adequately assessing the curriculum?

Reflection

- How will planning the year help you keep on track and focused?
- How will the curriculum map allow you to develop more reliable activities and assessments?
- How has creating a map allowed you to evaluate the standards?
- How will you ensure that critical thinking skills are embedded in your curriculum?

Resources

Ainsworth, L. (2003). *Power standards: Identifying the standards that matter the most*. Englewood, CO: Advanced Learning Press.

Ainsworth, L. (2003). *"Unwrapping" the standards: A simple process to make standards manageable.* Englewood, CO: Advanced Learning Press.

Erickson, H. L. (1988). *Concept-based curriculum and instruction: Teaching beyond facts*. Thousand Oaks, CA: Corwin Press.

Jacobs, H. H. (1997). *Mapping the big picture: Integrating curriculum and assessment K-12.* Alexandria, VA: ASCD Publications.

Resources *(continued)*

Saphier, J., & Gower, R. (1997). *The skillful teacher.* Acton, MA: Research on Better Teaching.

Wiggins, G., & McTighe, J. (1998). *Understanding by design*. Alexandria, VA: ASCD Publications.

Standards and Resources

WEEK 7

If you hate standards, learn to love the bell curve.

—Douglas Reeves (2002)

Action

Make a list of the resources you feel you will need to most effectively teach the curriculum this year. Visit the professional library for your district; you may want to go with another team member. Identify the resources available to you to teach a lesson.

Reflection

- What information were you able to gather about resources available to you?
- How will you use these district resources?
- How will these resources enable you to teach to the standards?
- What other resources will you need to be effective?

Generate some ideas so that you can procure the resources needed.

Resources

Ainsworth, L. (2003). *Power standards: Identifying the standards that matter the most.* Englewood, CO: Advanced Learning Press.

Ainsworth, L. (2003). *"Unwrapping" the standards: A simple process to make standards manageable.* Englewood, CO: Advanced Learning Press.

Reeves, D. (2002). *Making standards work: How to implement standards-based assessments in the classroom, school, and district.* Englewood, CO: Advanced Learning Press.

Communication of Standards

WEEK

8

Teach for accomplishment, using structured assignments with objectives and not only will the students demonstrate competence, but you will be regarded as a competent teacher also.

—Harry K. Wong (2005)

Action

Examine your grade book.

- How are you communicating standards to your students?
- How are you tracking progress toward meeting standards?

Reflection

- How can I help my students and their parents understand what the standards mean for them?
- How can I ensure that the district standards are rigorous enough?
- How can I ensure that the curriculum continues to be dynamic and still meet the standards?

Resources

Ainsworth, L. (1997). *Student generated rubrics.* Englewood, CO: Advanced Learning Press.

Guskey, T. (1996). *Communicating student learning: 1996 yearbook for ASCD.* Alexandria, VA: ASCD Publications.

Guskey, T., & Bailey, J. (2000). *Developing grading and reporting systems for student learning.* Alexandria, VA: ASCD Publications.

Marzano, R. (2000). *Transforming classroom grading.* Alexandria, VA: ASCD Publications.

Wong, H. K., & Wong, R. T. (2005). *The first days of school.* Mountain View, CA: Harry K. Wong Publications.

Verbal Feedback

WEEK 9

I have come to a frightening conclusion.
I am the decisive element in the classroom.
It is my personal approach that creates the climate.
It is my daily mood that makes the weather.
As a teacher I possess tremendous power to make a child's life miserable or joyous.
I can be a tool of torture or an instrument of inspiration.
I can humiliate or humor, hurt or heal.
In all situations it is my response that decides whether a crisis will be escalated or de-escalated, and a child humanized or dehumanized.

—Haim Ginot (1975)

Action

Read the following ways to respond to incorrect answers.

- If the answer is incomplete, provide a hint or clue.
- Rephrase the question in case it was not understood.
- Supply the correct answer and discuss it with the student.
- Give examples of possible answers in a positive way.
- Tell the student where the answer may be found.
- Ask the student to determine the question that he or she actually answered.
- Ask a classmate to determine the question that the student answered.
- Next time, after questioning allow "wait time" for all students to think.
- State reasons that the answer seemed logical.
- Ask the student to explain his or her reasoning.

Reflection

- Which of the preceding responses are you most comfortable with?
- Which have you not tried?

Reflection *(continued)*

Make an effort to incorporate all these strategies when assisting your students.

Resources

Bloom's Taxonomy (in, e.g., Ainsworth, L. (2003). *"Unwrapping" the standards: A simple process to make standards manageable.* Englewood, CO: Advanced Learning Press.

Freiberg, H. J., & Driscoll, A. (2000). *Universal teaching strategies.* Needham Heights, MA: Allyn & Bacon.

Ginot, H. (1975). *Between teacher and child.* New York: Simon & Schuster.

Saphier, J., & Gower, R. (1997). *The skillful teacher.* Acton, MA: Research on Better Teaching.

Planning Lessons

WEEK

10

An education isn't how much you have committed to memory, or even how much you know. It's being able to differentiate between what you know and what you don't.

—Anatole France (in Paris & Ayres, 1994)

Action

Select one of the questions from the following "Reflection" section and make a concerted effort to incorporate your answer into your lesson plans in a thoughtful and methodical manner this week.

Reflection

- How long does it take to plan a week's worth of lessons?
- Have you developed both a pre- and a post-assessment?
- Have you taken the time to find a way to "grab" students' attention?
- Can your lessons be easily modified as needed?
- Are you including a variety of instructional strategies?
- Are your lessons linked to previous learning?
- Are your lessons interdisciplinary?

Revisit this week's list from time to time.

Resources

Erickson, H. L. (1988). *Concept-based curriculum and instruction: Teaching beyond facts.* Thousand Oaks, CA: Corwin Press.

Freiberg, H. J., & Driscoll, A. (2000). *Universal teaching strategies.* Needham Heights, MA: Allyn & Bacon.

Marzano, R., & Pickering, D. (2001). *Classroom instruction that works: Research-based strategies for increasing student achievement.* Alexandria, VA: ASCD Publications.

Paris, S. G., & Ayres, L. R. (1994). *Becoming reflective students and teachers.* Washington, DC: American Psychological Association.

Resources *(continued)*

Saphier, J., & Gower, R. (1997). *The skillful teacher.* Acton, MA: Research on Better Teaching.

Wiggins, G., & McTighe, J. (1998). *Understanding by design.* Alexandria, VA: ASCD Publications.

Wong, H. K., & Wong, R. T. (2005). *The first days of school.* Mountain View, CA: Harry K. Wong Publications.

WEEK

11

Design—(verb): To have purposes and intentions; to plan and execute.

—Oxford English Dictionary

Action

After delivering a lesson to your students, sit and watch them work. What indicators of understanding do your students show you?

Reflection

- How do you ensure that your students will be successful?
- How do you know your students are learning?

Resources

Ferguson, D., & Ginevra, R. (2001). *Designing personalized learning for every student.* Alexandria, VA: ASCD Publications.

Gregory, G. & Chapman, C. (2002). *Differentiated instructional strategies.* Thousand Oaks, CA: Corwin Press.

Jones, B., Valdez, G., Nowakowski, J., & Rasmussen, C. (1994). *Designing learning and technology for educational reform.* Oak Brook, IL: North Central Regional Educational Laboratory.

Lazear, D. (1999). *Eight ways of knowing: Teaching for multiple intelligences.* Arlington Heights, IL: SkyLight Publishing.

WEEK

12

All big things in this world are done by people who are naive and have an idea that is obviously impossible.

—Frank Richards

Action

Visit a district board meeting. Collect the board agenda and add to your reflections.

Reflection

- What issues were addressed at the meeting?
- What did the board discuss?
- Did you have an opinion on the issues discussed?
- How will those issues affect your classroom?
- What insights has this activity provided you?

Resources

Danielson, C. (2002). *Enhancing student achievement: A framework for school improvement.* Alexandria, VA: ASCD Publications.

Hammond, L. (1997). *The right to learn: A blueprint for creating schools that work.* San Francisco, CA: Jossey-Bass.

Marzano, R. (2002–2003). *What works in schools: Translating research into action.* Alexandria, VA: ASCD Publications.

Reeves, D. (2000). *Accountability in action.* Englewood, CO: Advanced Learning Press.

Reeves, D. (2001). *101 questions & answers about standards, assessment, and accountability.* Englewood, CO: Advanced Learning Press.

Schmoker, M. (1999). Results: *The key to continuous school improvement.* Alexandria, VA: ASCD Publications.

WEEK

13

Each place along the way is somewhere you had to be to be here.
—Wayne W. Dyer

Action

Culture is the often unspoken set of norms, values, beliefs, traditions, and rituals that identify a group, organization, or society. According to Kent Peterson, the school culture can be inspirational or it can be toxic (Deal & Peterson, 2003).

Reflection

Select a staff member whom you believe has the ability to inspire. Make it a point to share your thoughts about this person and write a paragraph regarding his or her reaction, as well as your own thoughts.

Resources

Deal, T., & Peterson, K. (2003). *Shaping school culture: The heart of leadership.* San Francisco, CA: Jossey-Bass.

DuFour, R., Eaker, R., & Baker, R. (1998). *Professional learning communities at work: Best practice for enhancing student achievement.* Bloomington, IN: National Education Service.

Fullan, M. (2001). *Leading in a culture of change.* San Francisco, CA: Jossey-Bass.

Schein, E. H. (1992). *Organizational culture and leadership.* San Francisco, CA: Jossey-Bass.

Understanding

WEEK 14

There are many different ways of understanding, overlapping but not reducible to one another and, correspondingly, many different ways of teaching to understanding.

—J. Passmore (1982)

Action

Think about your past learning experiences. Can you recall a lesson you learned either in school or in life? Chances are you are fondly recalling a wonderful experience you had.

Reflection

Now think about what the elements of the lesson were. Try to take personalities out of the equation. A charismatic teacher may have made the lesson memorable, but think about what you "did" in the lesson. What actions did you take that helped you to feel so successful? See if you can come up with a list of five things that made the lesson effective.

Now, reflect on your own class:

- Do you provide those "things" for your students?
- How have you engaged your students in learning?

Resources

Erickson, H. L. (1988). *Concept-based curriculum and instruction: Teaching beyond facts.* Thousand Oaks, CA: Corwin Press.

Passmore, J. (1982). *The philosophy of teaching.* Cambridge, MA: Harvard University Press.

Wiggins, G., & McTighe, J. (1998). *Understanding by design.* Alexandria, VA: ASCD Publications.

WEEK

15

Strange as it may sound, students often will not know the purpose of a particular assessment unless teachers tell them directly—this rarely happens.

—Jon Saphier and Robert Gower (1997)

Action

During the week, keep track of the assessment(s) you do in your classroom. Make a list of the assessments and which standard(s) each aligns to. At the end of the week, analyze the information and describe what information you gathered about students' progress toward meeting the standards. Be sure to analyze the effectiveness of each type of assessment and how accurately (or not) it reflects student achievement.

- Are the assessments reliable?
- How do you know?

Reflection

- How will I determine which assessment methods are appropriate for a particular lesson?
- When I examine an assessment that is part of published materials I use, how will I judge whether to use it?
- Why is it important for me to use assessment data to make instructional decisions?

Resources

Center for Performance Assessment. (2001). *Performance assessment series: Classroom tips and tools for busy teachers* (Elementary and Middle School ed.). Englewood, CO: Advanced Learning Press.

Freiberg, H. J., & Driscoll, A. (2000). *Universal teaching strategies.* Needham Heights, MA: Allyn & Bacon.

Saphier, J., & Gower, R. (1997). *The skillful teacher.* Acton, MA: Research on Better Teaching.

Wiggins, G., & McTighe, J. (1998). *Understanding by design.* Alexandria, VA: ASCD Publications.

Assessments and Rubrics

WEEK

16

The rubric thus becomes a kind of road map, guiding [students] to their goal—a finished project that earned the grade they envisioned.

—Larry Ainsworth (1997)

Action

Using either a district rubric or a commercially developed rubric, practice using rubrics with your students.

Create a rubric for use this week. You may choose to use a procedural rubric, a content rubric, or a generic rubric. Describe how you developed the rubric, how you communicated the rubric to your class, and how your class performed based on the rubric.

Reflection

Reflect on the use of rubrics in your classroom and with your students.

- What were the results from using the rubric?
- How did your students react?
- How was their performance based on the rubric? Do you feel it improved the quality of their work?

Resources

Ainsworth, L. (1997). *Student generated rubrics.* Englewood, CO: Advanced Learning Press.

Arter, J., & McTighe, J. (2000). *Assessment as learning: Using classroom assessment to maximize student learning.* Thousand Oaks, CA: Corwin Press.

WEEK

17

Instructional units that shed a conceptual lens on a topic of study force thinking to the integration level. It is the conceptual focus that achieves this goal of integrated curriculum. Without the focus concept, we are merely "coordinating" facts and activities to a topic and we fail to reach higher-level curricular and cognitive integration.

—H. Lynn Erickson (1998)

Action

Make a list of concepts that connect to a unit of study you are teaching. *Concepts* are universal terms that can be used and applied across subject areas. For example, the concept of "systems" can be used in science (ecosystems, body systems), social studies (systems of government, cultural systems), mathematics (mathematical systems), and language arts (story as a system of elements).

Post a list of three concepts that you may consider using and explain the connections they would create across different disciplines. Create your own graphic organizer of one of the concepts.

Reflection

Select a concept that you will use to teach a topic to your students. For example, if the topic is butterflies, your concept might be life cycles and how caterpillars change through a gradual cycle into butterflies. Create an engaging learning activity that allows students to explore the concept you have chosen. How would you vary instructional strategies, resources, and materials in response to student differences?

Resources

Erickson, H. L. (1988). *Concept-based curriculum and instruction: Teaching beyond facts.* Thousand Oaks, CA: Corwin Press.

Marzano, R., & Pickering, D. (2001). *Classroom instruction that works: Research-based strategies for increasing student achievement.* Alexandria, VA: ASCD Publications.

Tomlinson, C. (2001). *How to differentiate instruction in mixed ability classrooms.* Alexandria, VA: ASCD Publications.

Wiggins, G., & McTighe, J. (1998). *Understanding by design.* Alexandria, VA: ASCD Publications.

WEEK

18

Variety is the spice of life.

Action

Look at your lesson plan book for the week.

Reflection

List the teaching strategies you used with your students this week. Next to the list, make a column to indicate if you were taught this way, and if this is an innovative strategy, a cooperative learning strategy, or a teacher-directed strategy.

- What does your graph say about the way you teach?
- Is it the same every day?
- Is there variety?

Resources

Johnson, D., & Johnson, R. (1999). *Learning together and alone: Warm-ups, grouping strategies, and grouping activities.* Needham Heights, MA: Allyn & Bacon.

Joyce, B. (2003). *Models of teaching.* Boston: Allyn & Bacon.

Marzano, R. (2001). *A handbook for classroom instruction that works.* Alexandria, VA: ASCD Publications.

WEEK

19

How to tell students what to look for without telling them what to see is the dilemma of teaching.

—Lascelles Abercrombie

Action

Synectics, concept attainment, Socratic seminar, inquiry, group investigation . . . any of these sound familiar?

Reflection

Any one of these strategies can be used effectively with students of all ages. Select one and explore. How can you develop a unit or a lesson using your chosen strategies?

Resources

Joyce, B. (2003). *Models of teaching: Concept attainment.* Boston: Allyn & Bacon.

Joyce, B. (2003). *Models of teaching: Synectics: The development of creative capacity*. Boston: Allyn & Bacon.

Saphier, J., & Gower, R. (1997). *The skillful teacher.* Acton, MA: Research on Better Teaching.

WEEK

20

If we knew we were on the right road, having to leave it would mean endless despair. But we are on a road that only leads to a second one and then to a third one and so forth. And the real highway will not be sighted for a long, long time, perhaps never. So we drift in doubt. But also in an unbelievable beautiful diversity. Thus the accomplishment of hopes remains an always unexpected miracle. But in compensation, the miracle remains forever possible.

—Franz Kafka

Action

What do you think are your talents or authentic gifts? Make a list of at least five qualities that make you a wonderful, unique person.

Reflection

- How are you using those qualities in your work and your life right now?
- How could you better use them in the future?

Resources

Breathhach, S. (1995). *Simple abundance: A daybook of comfort and joy.* New York: Warner Books.

Canfield, J., & Hansen, M. (2002). *Chicken soup for the soul.* Deerfield Beach, FL: Health Communications.

Norfolk, D. (2002). *The soul garden: Creating green spaces for inner growth and spiritual renewal.* Woodstock, NY: Overlook Press.

WEEK

21

When we value only restricted ways of learning, behaving and attending—especially high-stakes-test learning, sit-down-in-your-seat-and-look-at-the-blackboard behaving, and focus-on-the-vocabulary-word attending—then we ignore, stifle, or repress the other marvelous things that a student's brain might be capable of doing.

—Thomas Armstrong

Action

Read the individual education plan (IEP) of an identified special education student in your classroom. Were you involved with the staffing? Provide a brief student profile.

Reflection

Reflect on the following scenarios:

- On your first day at XYZ School, you notice that a substantial number of students with IEPs are assigned to your third-hour class. What is your legal responsibility in meeting the needs of these students?
- A special education teacher will assist you in the regular classroom with a number of students who have IEPs. What are your professional responsibilities and your ethical obligations in forging this partnership?
- You are asked to assist in the evaluation of a student who is referred for possible special education services. As a regular classroom teacher, what are your responsibilities in this evaluation process?
- What are your responsibilities regarding a student on a 504 plan?
- Write a brief profile for the student featured in your lesson plan. If you have no special needs students, ask your special education teacher for an example of a student profile.
- Using either an existing lesson plan or a newly written lesson plan, make the necessary adjustments for a special education student as referenced in the student's IEP. Your instructional strategies should indicate the adjustments you make for the student.

- Work with your special education teacher as you modify your lesson plans.

Resources

Hallahan, D, & Kaufman, J. (1999). *Exceptional learners: Introduction to special education.* Needham Heights, MA: Allyn & Bacon.

Rose, D., & Meyer, A. (2002). *Teaching every student in the digital age: Universal design for learning.* Alexandria, VA: ASCD Publications.

Shaywitz, S. (2003). *Overcoming dyslexia.* New York: Alfred A. Knopf.

WEEK

22

Push me! See how far I go!
Work me 'til I drop. Then pick me up.
Open a door, and then make me run to it before it closes.
Teach me so that I might learn,
Then let me enter the tunnel of experience alone.
And when, near the end,
I turn to see you beginning another's journey
I shall smile.

—14-year-old Kathleen

Action

An eighth-grade student spends time in his math class struggling with his multiplication. Next to him is a student who manages to attend class two or three times a week. Between the two is a math whiz, but it takes him the entire period to respond to a word problem because he is not a native English speaker. Sound familiar? Establishing a differentiated classroom can work to meet the needs of all the students in your class. Think about the students in your class.

Reflection

"In a differentiated classroom, the teacher proactively plans and carries out varied approaches to content, process, and product in anticipation of and response to students' differences in readiness, interest, and learning needs" (Tomlinson, 1999). According to Carol Ann Tomlinson, a teacher can differentiate by content, process, or product. *Content differentiation* consists of the use of different materials. *Process differentiation* implies that a teacher compacts or changes the curriculum. Finally, the *differentiation of product* allows learning to be demonstrated through various assessments.

Using the information presented in one of the resources, how would you differentiate a lesson you will be teaching over the next two weeks? Share your results with a colleague.

Resources

Ferguson, D., & Ralph, G. (2001). *Designing personalized learning for every student.* Alexandria, VA: ASCD Publications.

Tomlinson, C. (1999). *The differentiated classroom: Responding to the needs of all learners.* Alexandria, VA: ASCD Publications.

Tomlinson, C. (2001). *How to differentiate instruction in mixed ability classrooms.* Alexandria, VA: ASCD Publications.

Meeting the Needs of All Learners

WEEK

23

All big things in this world are done by people who are naive and have an idea that is obviously impossible.

—Frank Richard

Action

Bloom's Taxonomy. Multiple intelligences. The list goes on and on. It's everywhere, in books, in journals, in college classes: *We must meet the needs of all learners.* This is, in fact, the most difficult classroom challenge for a teacher. There are as many needs as there are students in your class. The optimum is to learn to use multiple strategies within each single lesson.

Reflection

This week, select and think about one student who often "doesn't get it." With this student in mind as you work on your lesson plans, include his or her interests as examples. Address questions to this student at his or her Bloom's level. Modify assignments as needed. Did you see a difference in this student?

Resources

Bloom's Taxonomy.

Tomlinson, C. (1999). *The differentiated classroom: Responding to the needs of all learners.* Alexandria, VA: ASCD Publications.

Tomlinson, C. (2001). *How to differentiate instruction in mixed ability classrooms.* Alexandria, VA: ASCD Publications.

WEEK

24

Students need frequent feedback about their performance as compared to clear, objective standards—not as compared with the performance of their peers. Students should not have to guess what individual teachers want from them in order to be successful, but should know exactly what they must do in order to achieve at high levels.

—Douglas Reeves (2004)

Action

For feedback to be meaningful, it must be genuine and timely. Think about how you provide feedback to your students.

Reflection

Now reflect on the following questions:

- Why do you assign homework?
- Does all homework get graded?
- Is homework returned to students in a timely manner?
- How do you reinforce appropriate and discourage inappropriate behavior?
- Do you personalize notes on assignments?
- Do you leave notes on assignments indicating that you know the effort was made although the assignment has to be reworked?

Resources

Guskey, T. (1996). *Communicating student learning: 1996 yearbook for ASCD*. Alexandria, VA: ASCD Publications.

Guskey, T., & Bailey, J. (2000). *Developing grading and reporting systems for student learning*. Alexandria, VA: ASCD Publications.

Marzano, R. (2000). *Transforming classroom grading*. Alexandria, VA: ASCD Publications.

Reeves, D. (2004). *Accountability in action*. Englewood, CO: Advanced Learning Press.

WEEK 25

Computers will make a difference not only in the way kids learn but also in the way their brains approach information processing.

—Jane M. Healey

Action

Seek out your building instructional technology (IT) person. If you don't have an IT person in your building, find out if your district has someone who can be of assistance. Meet with this person to find out the resources available to you.

Technology can be incorporated in many forms. You may use the technology to instruct: use a PowerPoint presentation, a SMART board, a computerized assessment system. You may incorporate technology for the students: the use of computer software such as PowerPoint, Web searching, digital storytelling, and so on. Choose one way in which you will incorporate technology into your instruction and design a lesson.

Reflection

- How did the students respond to the lesson?
- Were you able to effectively instruct students?
- What will you need to do in the future to make technology an integral part of your instruction?

Resources

Brooks-Young, S. (2002). *Making technology standards work for you: A guide for school administrators.* Eugene, OR: International Society for Technology in Education.

Jonassen, D., et al. (1998). *Learning with technology: A constructivist perspective.* Englewood Cliffs, NJ: Prentice-Hall.

November, A. (2001). *Empowering students with technology.* Glenview, IL: Skylight Publishing.

Communicating with Parents

WEEK

26

If you don't give people information, they'll make it up to fill the void.

—Carla O'Dell

Action

Take a look at the communications that went home with students this school year. Review your "welcome" letter, newsletters, cards, and memos that you received from parents as well as any special communications you sent to them. Make sure you include your telephone log. Most importantly, take a look at the *types* of communications you sent home to parents. All parents like to receive something positive about their children, but all too frequently a large percentage of our time is spent informing parents of the negative.

Advice

- Have someone proofread written communications that go to students' homes.
- Consider sending a newsletter as a team, by grade level.

Reflection

- What percentage of your communications to parents were positive?
- What percentage were negative?
- What can you do to increase the number of positive communications that go home?

Resources

Freiberg, H. J., & Driscoll, A. (2000). *Universal teaching strategies.* Needham Heights, MA: Allyn & Bacon.

Guskey, T. (1996). *Communicating student learning: 1996 yearbook for ASCD.* Alexandria, VA: ASCD Publications.

Marzano, R. (2000). *Transforming classroom grading.* Alexandria, VA: ASCD Publications.

WEEK

27

It takes all of us . . . for the woods would be very silent if no birds sang but the best.

—Henry VanDyke

Action

Find an article, a book, a great lesson plan, a technology strategy, or an idea and share it with a colleague with whom you do not normally interact. Generate a couple of questions about the item and ask your colleague for his or her input.

Sit next to someone with whom you do not usually sit during a staff meeting, and generate a conversation about a student the two of you share.

Ask a veteran teacher if you may observe in her or his classroom and gain some ideas; then ask if you can spend 15 minutes with her or him and debrief your findings or ask questions about the strategies you observed.

Reflection

Describe the reaction from each setting.

- What did you gain?
- Has the collegiality improved?

Resources

Freiberg, H. J., & Driscoll, A. (2000). *Universal teaching strategies.* Needham Heights, MA: Allyn & Bacon.

Periodicals

Educational Leadership, a magazine for educators by educators, is ASCD's flagship publication. With a circulation of 175,000, *Educational Leadership* is acknowledged throughout the world as an authoritative source of information about teaching and learning, new ideas and practices relevant to practicing educators, and the latest trends and issues affecting prekindergarten through higher education.

Education Week, American education's newspaper of record, provides weekly news along with timely, objective, and comprehensive reports on the trends and developments affecting schools and the people who staff them.

Phi Delta Kappan, the professional print journal for education, addresses policy issues for educators at all levels. Advocating research-based school reform, the *Kappan* provides a forum for debate on controversial subjects. Published since 1915, the journal appears monthly September through June.

Motivation

WEEKS 28 and 29

To know how to suggest is the great art of teaching. . . . we must learn to read the child's soul as we might a piece of music. Then, by simply changing the key, we keep up the attraction and vary the song.

—Henri Frederic Amiel

Action

Think about the students in your class. Divide the group into three categories: self-motivated, happy to comply, and unmotivated.

Reflection

Reflect on one of your students from the unmotivated list. How will you motivate this student in the future? Develop a plan of action you will use to help this student achieve in your classroom. You may decide to use some incentive(s), you may need to develop a learning contract, or you may just need to set the expectation for this individual—be creative! This journal should demonstrate reflection about a particular student and your plan of action to try to meet the individual needs of that student.

You may want to include the following:

- Did you communicate the plan to the student? If so, how?
- Describe how the student reacted to the new plan of action.
- Did you solicit support from the administration, home, or other students?
- How did you decide on this plan of action?

Resources

Rogers, S., Ludington, J., & Graham, S. (1999). *Motivation and learning*. Evergreen, CO: Peak Learning Systems.

WEEK

30

Schools exist to promote student achievement. In that sense, it is the most valued outcome of schools. If students achieve, schools are seen as working effectively. Grades are supposed to reflect a student's level of success in learning the required material.

—Rick Stiggins

Action

Set up a time to speak to a colleague who teaches the same content or at the same grade level. Center your discussion around these points:

- Is your grading aligned to performance standards?
- Is your report card equipped to handle the performance standards indicators, such as "exceeds," "meets," or "does not meet" the standard?
- Do you and your colleague have samples of student work that show growth?
- Is your colleague using rubrics? Are you?
- Do you return all assignments to your students with indicators that you have reviewed the work?

Reflection

How will your grading system change to reflect the outcome of your discussion of all the preceding points?

Resources

Guskey, T. (1996). *Communicating student learning: 1996 yearbook for ASCD*. Alexandria, VA: ASCD Publications.

Guskey, T., & Bailey, J. (2000). *Developing grading and reporting systems for student learning*. Alexandria, VA: ASCD Publications.

Marzano, R. (2000). *Transforming classroom grading*. Alexandria, VA: ASCD Publications.

WEEK

31

If you always do what you've always done, you'll always get what you always got.

—Ed Foreman

Action

Make a list of the staff development opportunities available to you this year. You may want to talk with your mentor or administrator. Decide which staff development you will attend this year and how you hope it will improve your teaching.

Reflection

- Does your professional portfolio provide evidence of your continued learning? How does it show this?
- Does it show the effects this learning has had on student achievement?

Resources

Brown, J., & Moffet, C. (1999). *The hero's journey: How educators can transform schools and improve learning*. Alexandria, VA: ASCD Publications.

Danielson, C. (1996). *Enhancing professional practice: A framework for teaching*. Alexandria, VA: ASCD Publications.

Sargent, J., & Smejkal, A. (2000). *Targets for teachers: A self-study guide for teachers in the age of standards.* Winnipeg, Canada: Portage & Main Press.

The Change Process

WEEK

32

If you're not working in company that is enthusiastic, energetic, creative, clever, curious, and just plain fun, you've got trouble, serious trouble.

—Tom Peters (1998)

Action

Take an honest look at yourself. Is change difficult for you? Does change come easily? For most people, change is difficult; it is unfamiliar and not understood. We often dig our heels in and defy anyone who attempts to interject something new.

Reflection

When something new is introduced, is your response:

- "Tell me more—how will this fit with what I am already doing"?
- "Why? What I'm doing is good enough"?

Resources

Fullan, M. (2001). *Leading in a culture of change.* San Francisco, CA: Jossey-Bass.

Peters, T. (1998). *In search of excellence.* New York: Warner Books.

Saphier, J., & Gower, R. (1997). *The skillful teacher.* Acton, MA: Research on Better Teaching.

Schein, E. H. (1992). *Organizational culture and leadership.* San Francisco, CA: Jossey-Bass.

WEEK

33

Albert Schweitzer was a brilliant organist, musicologist, theologian, and philosopher. At the age of 30 he gave up promising careers and entered medical school in order to go to equatorial Africa as a doctor. Throughout his life he continued to learn and grow with every book he wrote, with every organ piece he played, and with every encounter he had both in Europe and in Africa. He never stopped learning.

—A. Schweitzer (1998)

Action

List classes and activities that you plan to pursue to keep you a lifelong learner.

Reflection

- How will you pass the love of learning on to your students?
- What learnings are you passionate about?
- What do you read?
- What topics are discussed when you gather with colleagues?

Resources

Schweitzer, A. (1998). *Out of my life and thought: An autobiography.* Baltimore, MD: Johns Hopkins University Press.

WEEK 34

Experience can be attained by you . . . .
Care more than others think is wise . . . .
Risk more than others think is safe . . . .
Dream more than others think is practical . . . .
Expect more than others think is possible.

—Author unknown

Action

Take a look around your faculty. Is there someone you admire because of how she or he speaks, acts, dresses, asks questions, responds to questions, keeps on top of current research?

Reflection

- Are your thoughts organized and easily understood?
- Do your actions convey confidence?
- Is your dress appropriate?
- Are your questions well thought through? Are they too ambiguous to understand?
- Do you respond to questions appropriately? Do you ask for clarification if you do not understand them?
- Do you belong to a professional organization?
- Do you read educational journals, books, or magazines?
- Would you want your own child to be in your classroom?

Resources

Danielson, C. (1996). *Enhancing professional practice.* Alexandria, VA: ASCD Publications.

Wong, H. K., & Wong, R. T. (2005). *The first days of school.* Mountain View, CA: Harry K. Wong Publications.

WEEK

35

Lawyers and judges are more and more becoming a part of school life.

—Myra Pollack Sadker and David Miller Sadker (2000, pg. 352)

Action

Read the following and respond to questions.

Family Education Rights and Privacy Act (FERPA)

FERPA is a federal law designed to protect the privacy of a student's educational records. Parents or eligible students (18 years or older) have a right to inspect and review all of the student's educational records maintained by the school.

Parents and or eligible students have a right to request that a school correct records believed to be inaccurate or misleading. If the school refuses to change the records, the parent or eligible student may request a formal hearing. If after the hearing the school still refuses the correction[,] the parent or eligible student has the right to place a statement in the records commenting on the contested information.

Generally, the school must have written permission from the parent or eligible student before releasing information. However, the law allows schools to disclose records without consent to the following parties:

- School employees who have a need to know
- Other schools to which a student is transferring
- Parents when a student over 18 is still dependent
- Certain government officials in order to carry out lawful functions
- Appropriate parties in connection [with] financial aid to a student
- Organizations doing certain studies for a school

- Accrediting institutions
- Individuals who have obtained a court order or subpoena
- Persons who need to know in case of safety or health emergencies
- State and local authorities to whom disclosure is required by state laws adopted before November 19, 1994
- Schools may also disclose, without consent, "directory" type information such as a student's name, address, telephone number, date and place of birth, honors, awards, and dates of attendance

HOWEVER

The school must tell parents and [the] student of the information that is designated as directory information and provide a reasonable amount of time to allow parents or eligible students to request [that] the school not disclose the information.

Schools must notify parents and eligible students of this law. The actual means of notification is left to each school (special letter, inclusion in a newsletter, PTA bulletin, student handbook, newspaper article).

Schools (school districts) must adopt a written policy about complying with FERPA.

Reflection

- Can I post student grades by number?
- Can students grade one another's work?
- Can I require that students call out grades for me to record in my grade book?
- Can parent volunteers grade homework?
- Can I post a chart to track homework, such as multiplication tables?
- Can I post samples of student work?

Resources

Family Education Rights and Privacy Act of 1974, 20 U.S.C. § 1232g.

Sadker, M. P., & Sadker, D. M. (2000). *Teachers, schools, and society.* New York: McGraw-Hill.

WEEK

36

Ultimately, the hero's journey in education is a shared experience. It is an on-going event, a process in which the new and the old, the seasoned and the uninitiated, work together toward a common set of purposes. It is a journey, not the destination, that we all share as a part of the heroic quest in education.

—J. Brown and C. Moffet (1999)

Action

Most states address ethics and democracy in the classroom. Look up your state or district teacher standards and review the expectations.

Reflection

- Do you routinely address issues such as cheating?
- Do you provide opportunities for the democratic process to be used in your classroom?

Resources

Brown, J., & Moffet, C. (1999). *The hero's journey: How educators can transform schools and improve learning*. Alexandria, VA: ASCD Publications.

Dewey, J. (1997). *Education and democracy.* New York: Free Press.

District policy

State standards

Appendix: Types of Journal Responses

There are many ways to use a journal. It may be a place to write down all your emotions and feelings, a place you can vent your frustrations and revisit your joys. It may be a place where you can truly be honest with yourself. We choose to believe that it will be a way for you to encourage yourself to go a little deeper into your teaching, as you examine yourself in a safe and nurturing environment. It encourages you to become a colleague, mentor, and professional. Here are just a few ways you can structure your responses. Make this journal work for you and your lifestyle.

Types of Journals

Reflective Journal

Reflective Journal		
What happened?	How do I feel about it?	What did I learn?

Speculation about Effects Journal

This type of journal helps examine the long-term effects or consequences of events. This encourages teachers to anticipate the effects of the events experienced.

Speculation about Effects Journal	
What happened?	What could happen because of this?

Double-Entry Journal

This allows teachers to respond to text as they read. The left column is for recording a text that is intriguing or puzzling or connects to an idea. The right column is for recording the teacher's reaction to the text.

Double-Entry Journal	
Quotation—a phrase or sentence I especially liked	My thoughts on the quotation

Metacognitive Journal

Metacognition is a higher level of critical thinking that occurs when one is aware of the thought processes involved with reading. This type of journal encourages teachers to analyze their own thought processes following a reading or an activity.

Here are some essential questions to help guide this type of journal response:

- What enabled you to get the most from your experience?
- What would you do differently next time?

In the left column, teachers record what they learned; the right column is for describing how they learned it.

Metacognitive Journal	
What I learned	How I learned it

Synthesis Journal

Upon completion of a journal activity, a teacher could choose to synthesize the information. This journal response type requires the teacher to think of practical applications for the newly learned or newly discovered information.

Synthesis Journal		
What I did	What I learned	How can I use it?

Other Ideas or Guidelines for Journal Reponses

- Take time to brainstorm; just write down everything that comes to mind. Try to write your first thoughts so that you can later analyze why certain things stuck out in your mind.
- Make connections to your own experiences.
- Make connections with either text you have read or conversations you have had in the past.
- Ask yourself questions as you complete the journal responses. Try starters such as "I wonder why . . ." or "I was surprised to learn . . . ."
- Try to imagine yourself in someone else's shoes. How would you react? What would you do differently or similarly?
- Carry on a conversation with yourself.
- Really be open and honest with yourself about your feelings. You may be uncomfortable. Try to define why you feel the discomfort.